Quadrille de Monsieur de Guise

ROY

Quadrille de Monsieur.

Princely Feasts
and Festivals

BRYAN HOLME

Princely Feasts and Festivals

Five centuries of Pageantry and Spectacle

With 58 color illustrations

THAMES AND HUDSON

On the end-papers: "Le Grand Carozel Royal": contemporary
engraving showing the tournament held in Paris in June 1662

On the half-title: Louis XIV in ballet costume. Engraving in the
Bibliothèque Nationale, Paris

Frontispiece: celebrations for the wedding of the Dauphin to the
Infanta María Teresa of Spain in a theatre built in the Versailles
riding school, 1745

© 1988 Thames and Hudson Ltd, London

First published in the United States in 1988 by
Thames and Hudson Inc., 500 Fifth Avenue,
New York, New York 10110

Library of Congress Catalog Card Number 88-50132

Printed and bound in Hong Kong

A wedding feast, from 'Histoire du Grand Alexandre', French manuscript, c. 1454. Musée du Petit Palais, Paris

All now was turned to jollity and game,
To luxury and riot, feast and dance.

MILTON

HERE MUST HAVE BEEN A DAY, not too long after Eden, when man and woman first dressed themselves not just for warmth, but with an eye to charm, dazzle and captivate one another. The moment that happened style was born and with it the pageantry which throughout history has contributed as much to the success of a princely feast as the food itself.

It's a long jump from Eden to where this book starts in the fourteenth century AD, but virtually no contemporary European paintings of feasts and festivals are to be found before then, certainly no great masterpieces. While there are frequent references to feasts in the Bible, to get an idea, for example, of how Belshazzar might have looked at that riotous feast when he saw the writing on the wall, we find ourselves turning to Rembrandt's painting of the seventeenth century. And if searching for the earliest illustrations of Herod's party when Salome shed her seven veils, there is little chance of finding anything worth while before Benozzo Gozzoli's fifteenth century masterpiece. And so it goes.

Hints of revelry do appear in certain ancient murals and friezes, and on very many Attic vases and drinking vessels. A youth or maiden might be picking grapes, playing a musical instrument, dancing, or in other ways suggesting a feast to be at hand. Many of the classical Greek figures are lovely enough to have inspired tone poems, lyrical verse and dance, yet they remain but fragments of a long lost story.

During Europe's Middle Ages art was overwhelmingly religious, but by the fifteenth century many secular scenes including festivals are to be found (page 17).

The Renaissance artist's chief patron was the church; but increasingly there were others who provided him with a wider range of subject matter — noblemen, well-to-do merchants or, if he was lucky enough to be a Florentine, one of the Medici bankers. He might still undertake a 'Procession of the Magi' for a private chapel — as Gozzoli did in Piero de' Medici's palace — paint a family portrait, or undertake an allegory of 'Peace', 'Friendship' or perhaps 'The Triumph of Virtue over Vice'. Allegories also became themes for the masques, or pageant plays that were performed in Italy and later, more often, in England. These featured large pasteboard constructions of a fairytale castle, a fanciful ship, a 'Tower of Love' or other theme around which performers would sing, dance and act out a story — usually on Shrove Tuesday, Midsummer's Eve and throughout the twelve days of Christmas.

A number of Italian artists — Botticelli, Titian, Caravaggio and Pollaiuolo, for instance — spent much time in their studios interpreting the myths of Greece and Rome. With the scholarly revival of interest in antiquity, ancient mythology — along with astrology — had become a very popular study.

All these paintings of biblical and mythological stories and characters had, of course, to be based entirely on the artist's imagination, yet they have remained as the 'authentic' references. Few today would dare depart from tradition when producing a Nativity at Christmas time, when dressing a classic play, or an opera like *Salome*, and when designing a dress for a costume ball or *tableau vivant*.

A classic example of this tradition is to be found in the painting of the annual *Ommeganck* staged in Brussels' *Grande Place* in the year 1615 (pages 46–49). While the presentations were typical of festivals all over Europe, the size and scope of this canvas and the meticulous attention to detail make it remarkable. The themes were divided between religious and mythological pageants. In the former category were a 'Nativity' and 'Christ Among the Doctors', and in the latter, an 'Apollo and the Nine Muses', and 'Diana the Huntress with Nymphs'.

Apollo and Diana also turned up with other perennial favourites at costume balls. Louis XIV of France whose zodiac sign, Leo, according to the astrologers placed him under the rule of Apollo, took the ancient sun god so much to heart that there were times when the king all but claimed Apollo as his own creation (page 57). With the help of clever architects, Louis also brought the spirit of the classical fable alive through the interplay of golden rays of sunlight in the chapel at Versailles to which he would retreat every day. Majestic symbols of Apollo are also present in the famed sculptures and fountains of the palace gardens.

As history remembers Louis as the 'Sun King', so those at the court of his grandson remembered Madame d'Etoiles, later Marquise de Pompadour (page 75), as 'Diana', when she came as a radiant 'huntress' to the Yew Ball, or *Bal des*

Ifs, at Versailles in 1745 (page 76). Madame d'Etoiles had earlier remarked to a friend that the only man for whom she would ever give up her husband was the king himself. After chatting and dancing with her 'quarry', whom she had just then met for the first time, she was not only to become Louis XV's mistress, but a trusted and most able adviser in affairs of state until she died nineteen years later.

While princely costume balls and fêtes were filled with Apollos, Dianas, Aphrodites and mischievous nymphs, carnival time brought out a wider range of attractions. A popular standby was Richard Coeur de Lion with his Crusaders storming a castle of 'infidels'. Then there were the weird and wonderful floats purposely designed to draw shrieks of horror and delight from the happy crowds. One shocker might be a gorgon with human head and writhing vipers (activated by hidden strings) as hair; another the famous sea monster who rippled across the waves and would have devoured poor Andromeda, helplessly chained to a rock, had the valiant Perseus missed his cue.

At the festival in Siena's Piazza del Campo 'monsters' mingled with the bull- and bear-baiters, each ducking, rearing and prancing around the ring with two pairs of tell-tale human legs just, but only just, showing (page 38).

The most spectacular medieval sport was the joust (pages 18 and 39). This, besides being a regular entertainment at court, was staged with the greatest splendour during the long celebrations that would honour the engagement or marriage of some royal couple.

Stemming from a ruthless military tradition, the joust had, before the end of the fourteenth century, become not only a test of strength, but an exercise of fairness, honour and valour according to the strict rules of chivalry associated with the legendary Christian knights at the Court of King Arthur.

René of Anjou, the colourful poet, artist and king, who combined 'chivalric virtues and artistic prowess to the full', wrote the most detailed and beautifully illustrated treatise giving the rules and procedures of his favourite sport. This was in 1450, when jousting was at the very height of popularity. By the seventeenth century the joust had deteriorated into little more than a star turn at festivals with colourful knights (or actors) giving token performances as they moved along the procession of clowns, musicians, troubadours, tumblers, stilt-walkers, dwarfs, giants and other acts.

The crowning glory of a great national celebration was, as it still is, a giant firework display (pages 80–81). At Versailles, where the glittering court of Louis XIV, in its setting of unparalleled splendour, represented the best of everything, nothing was done by half measures. Louis often arranged many of the details of a display himself. With glee he would watch the fireworks as they whizzed, sputtered and burst into cascades of light while comfortably seated at a window in an upstairs suite in the palace. The window overlooked the vast pond or lake, on which – for his and his court's amusement – he would arrange mock battles, having transported large naval vessels untold distances to engage in heated exchanges of sham gunfire. The entire court – save for the valiants battling it out on the lake – would watch, gasp and applaud enthusiastically whenever the king did. This sometimes proved a good way for a courtier to be 'seen', and if favourably so, of being singled out to perform some mission or favour leading in turn to a promotion. But as Louis was once to remark when he granted a favour – 'I have made a hundred people jealous, and one ungrateful.'

Central to a festive day was the feast itself. On this occasion, as on all others, the sovereign was surrounded by courtiers and enjoyed no privacy at all. A number of interesting paintings have been made of kings 'dining in public', as on page 69.

At banquets, the 'upper crust', seated at the head of the table, were served the upper and most appetizing part of a loaf of bread, while those 'below the salt', seated at the side tables, got portions of the lesser prized half.

The dining hall was usually constructed with a minstrels' gallery where the musicians, at a signal from the head servitor, would rise to salute the arrival of each new course with a round of fanfares.

The customary menu consisted of at least three courses, each offering what in these days would seem to be a quite staggering quantity of dishes. In the fifteenth century there were a number of recipes long since omitted from cook books, with evocative and exotic names such as Nomblys de Roo, Pety perueis, Mammenye and Leche Lumbarde. The above could be added — along with bread, beer and wine — to make the following a fairly typical banquet. Meat (probably beef or venison) in pepper sauce or with mustard, capon, heron, swan, curlew, woodcock, pheasant, plover, partridge, larks, snipe — all usually roasted; swan pudding, eel in saffron sauce, herring milwel or ling tails, salmon, pike, plaice, sole, haddock, hake, poached minnows with fritters, pastries and strawberries to top things up.

It was not expected that any guest would tackle more than half the number of dishes, and one or two listed on such a menu might never be prepared. The etiquette was choice, and those unable to resist really stuffing themselves might taste an extra bit of this, that or another delicacy as it came around — rinsing sticky fingers in rose water proffered in a silver bowl by a servitor.

At the table of Henry VIII, quantity was all important, and following a big feast, the king had an equally healthy appetite for entertainment. Henry loved music no less than a pretty face, and on one occasion when Ann Boleyn, Queen Catherine of Aragon's lady-in-waiting, sang him one of the songs he himself had composed and with 'such utter sweetness' the fateful events so well recorded in history were already in the making.

In 1520 Henry met the French king Francis I, near Calais on 'The Field of the Cloth of Gold' (page 30), taking his queen, Catherine of Aragon, and thousands of courtiers, soldiers, servants and entertainers with him. It was the biggest festival of its kind in the century. Cardinal Wolsey was in overall charge of the catering and he worried himself almost sick about it. The page after page of provisions the Cardinal ordered ranged from 700 conger eels, 2014 sheep, 26 dozen heron and 4 bushels of mustard all the way down to one pound and one penny's worth of 'cream for the king's cakes'. It would have been almost more than Wolsey's life — or post — was worth to have forgotten the all important cream and cakes. The enormous and costly festivities were intended to reconcile the two countries after centuries of mutual mistrust and hatred. It was agreed on the grounds of safety that neither Henry nor the French king should take part in jousting, although it was one of Henry's favourite sports. But Henry, on the spur of the moment, could not resist challenging Francis to a wrestling match. Though the odds were on Henry gaining the upper hand, French history claims that it was Francis who threw the English king quite flat on his back. The incident was never recorded by the English. Whether true, half true or the idle boast of a French courtier, such was the underlying mood of suspicion and distrust of the French — who some English feared had arranged this whole affair on French soil simply as a booby trap — that the incident could have been enough to turn this historic peace meeting into a battleground. Luckily no such thing happened.

Although the English traditionally have always held their own more than well on the battleground, in politics, in literature and the theatre, they have always had to bow to the superiority of the French in matters of art, the elegance of female dress and the art of cooking. In no country but France would anyone have ever dreamed of trying to make anything as unpromising as frogs' legs and snails into first-rate delicacies, let alone to have been completely successful in doing so.

France owes some of its culinary supremacy to Catherine de Médicis (page 34) who, after marrying Henry II in Marseilles in 1533, brought Italian cooks and many superb Roman recipes with her, including possibly one for ice cream, never previously heard of north of the Alps. And it may have been through Catherine that the fork first appeared at the banquet table of her son Henry III.

In the reign of Louis XIV (when calories were unknown, let alone counted) the Duchess of Orleans attending a typical banquet at Versailles reported that the main meal was a quite important affair which would seem to have required the attendance of 498 employees of the Service de la Bouche (royal table). 'The king ate four plates of soup of different kinds, a whole pheasant, a partridge, a large plate of salad, two thick slices of ham, a dish of mutton in a garlic flavoured sauce, a plateful of pastries, and then fruit and hard boiled eggs'.

Louis XIV's grandson and heir to the throne, Louis XV, was an even more renowned gourmet than the Sun King and was most receptive to the many innovations in cooking that were developed during his reign. The Duc de Richelieu was to introduce *mahonnaise sauce*, or mayonnaise, with which the King then loved to smother a plate of eggs. Other delicacies carrying the name of the celebrity who created them were *Potage à la Condé, Poulets à la Villeroy, Chartreuses à la Mauconseil* and *Gigot à la Mailly*, names that French chefs have lovingly rolled off their tongues ever since. Louis was considerably more interested in his meals, in hunting or passing the time of day with carpenters, masons and locksmiths than he was in attempting to run the country. At a typical light lunch before a hunt, the king was reported to have downed 'four cutlets, a whole chicken, a plateful of ham, a half dozen eggs in sauce, and a bottle and a half of champagne' before heaving himself onto his horse and trotting off to *la chasse royale*.

In 1665 an English son of a cook, Robert May, wrote *The Accomplisht Cook*. In it he referred quite disparagingly to French cooking, implying that English cooking was as good as, if not rather better than, French; it was a patriotic thought at least. May also referred to 'the days wherein were produced the triumphs and trophies of cookery'.

While part of the attraction of a feast, or the hours following one, was music, dancing, and acting, the kitchen, with its 'triumphs' competed for the day's laurels. Heraldic devices, animals, castles, human figures — sometimes life-size — and other 'trophies' would be created out of marzipan and other hardy yet edible confections. The largest creations might decorate the hall, smaller ones a long table.

An extremely popular *tour de force* at a banquet was the peacock — not presented as a roasted corpse; on the contrary often so realistically re-dressed in its own iridescent feathers as to appear ready to rise out of its new nest of aspic and soar to the rafters. The real 'surprises' — although guests usually knew well what was coming — were the huge half-artificial cakes out of which, to the roll of drums or shrill trumpet blasts, would burst some comic or sprightly figure to mime, tease, sing or dance.

The old nursery rhyme *Sing a Song of Sixpence* was not all nonsense. The 'four and twenty blackbirds baked in a pie' were not in fact baked; only the crust of the pie was baked while the birds, probably fewer than twenty-four, poor things, were tethered inside. 'And when the pie was opened' was it really true that 'the birds began to sing'? They would most likely have been ready to hit the ceiling.

The size and splendour of a feast was an indication of nobility, wealth and 'divine' plenty. The responsibilities of serving the royal party at the head table were often filled by sons of noblemen who, while attentively doing so and learning all about etiquette and courtly behaviour, could lend an inquisitive ear to top level political discussions and gossip (page 17). And if the king liked his 'presence' and began to trust him he might soon find his star in ascendancy.

The hierarchy at court was based on the analogy of the heavens wherein the sun, shining in full glory, was surrounded by planets and stars of gradually diminishing importance. At court, these consisted of the rest of the royal family, grand ministers of the crown and state, high military and naval officers, lords and ladies in waiting, the grand masters of the dozens and dozens of different departments, each with first, second and third-in-line assistants, valets, cooks, bread carriers, on down to the last hardworking stable-boy or scullery-maid — the smallest but still sparkling star in the dizzy firmament.

To attend court, the hub of the nation's affairs and the centre of society, was often considered the obligation of the nobility. It was also the best possible finishing school, through which a distinguished marriage might result. Where else could a young man learn the royal pursuits of jousting, hunting, falconry, tilting, archery, and where else would he have the opportunity of attending theatre, opera (page 83), ballets, balls (page 50) and all the other glittering functions that the court could offer? Edmund Spenser once praised the royal court as being a unique means whereby 'to fashion a gentleman or noble in virtuous and noble discipline'. Another writer went as far as to call it 'the most glamorous existence anyone not destined for the life of an ecclesiast or aesthete could ask for'.

By no means, however, could life at court have been a bed of roses. Sydney Anglo, basing his summary of the 'ideal courtier' on an early seventeenth century text by Louis Guyon, writes that he should be skilful in wrestling, leaping, dancing and playing on some or many instruments of music, so should he likewise readily sing any poet or historian. He must be a linguist; a fluent conversationalist; witty but not offensive. His behaviour toward his prince must be attentive but not servile; he must wait for favours, not demand them; and he must never insinuate himself by 'serving in murderous or bawdy employments'. He should dress soberly; avoid gaming and drunkenness; and engage in amorous pursuits only with propriety and decorum. All these qualities are to be employed to gain favour, so that the courtier can become a trusted adviser, able to express truth without fear. A virtuous courtier makes a virtuous prince, whereas a vicious courtier makes his prince wicked and detestable, for to succeed at court where there are bullies and flatterers and where virtue is mocked, a man must be corrupt; to become rich he must, among other things, be prepared to lie, cheat, slander and drink.

William of Malmesbury, writing in the Middle Ages, saw nothing but the odious side of court life. For him the court was 'a death in life, a hell on earth'. Another anti-court author concluded that it was 'a dangerous place of discomfort, iniquity, vice', and in the opinion of a more recent critic it was at its very best 'a hothouse for the developing of the full-time dilettante'.

But for all the inevitable intrigues, jealousies, briberies, hypocrisies, cruelty, amorous frustrations, heartaches and even at times, abject boredom, there were golden days for the lucky.

Imagine the excitement of dressing up with the whole court to be a leading equestrian at the most glamorous carousel in history (page 54), or being the Master of the Revels at the court of Elizabeth I, the 'Sun Queen' (page 36), who maintained singers, vocalists and over sixty instrumentalists. Despite the cries of the Puritans who frowned on plays as idolatrous, unseemly, 'bawdy fables', Elizabeth continued her patronage of the theatre and one year arranged for as many as ten plays to be presented at court. She attended the premiere of the promising young William Shakespeare's *A Comedy of Errors*, escorted by her current favourite, the Earl of Essex, and later the first performance of *A Midsummer Night's Dream*, as guest of honour, during the celebrations surrounding the marriage of the Earl of Derby to Lady Elizabeth Vere.

Elizabeth's great love of the theatre led her to form her own company in 1583 under the name of 'Queen Elizabeth's men'. It consisted of twelve members – the best actors 'borrowed' from the existing London companies, including the famous comedian Richard Tarleton. They received a salary for performances at court, and royal patronage proved helpful against the hostile authorities of the City of London. In the intervals of seasons in the capital they travelled all over the country.

The queen reserved her personal conquests in the country for her annual pilgrimage or 'royal progress' during which she would meet and talk to her more distant subjects in the towns and villages she passed through, increasing her enormous popularity. Frequently she invited herself and half her court to visit a friend like William Cecil or Christopher Hatton, causing complete and utter consternation. The alarm was caused not only by the bankrupting expense of a royal visit – refurbishing the stately mansion, buying chairs, tapestries and laying in mammoth provisions – but also of finding accommodation for everyone without resorting to too many haylofts or smelly stables – not to mention a 'suitable' berth for Sir Walter Raleigh or some other favourite her majesty might decide to bring with her at the last moment.

During Elizabeth's 1591 'progress' in Hampshire, Sir Henry Lee, whose trusted servant one night had failed to find anywhere for him to lay his weary head, complained 'I am old and come now evil away with the miseries of progress'.

Royal progresses, and even more so, 'royal entries' took enormous planning. These state visits often involved a long journey over bumpy and sometimes muddy roads, with a large percentage of the court in attendance, including as many royal and political dignitaries as possible, courtiers, military escorts, musicians and actors together with the usual retinue of helpers, servants and cartloads of provisions. Everyone was at hand, and dressed in their elegant best (page 58). As the town to be visited would stage a big flag-waving reception and feast, the royal 'entry' had to live up to the expectations of the citizens, presenting a royal, glittering spectacle, large and magnificent enough for them to remember and talk about for the rest of their lives. About the same amount of effort, perhaps more, went into the preparations of all the pageantry surrounding a royal wedding or, the biggest event of all, a coronation.

Any of the famous coronations in history are likely to have been described by local historians or reporters as the biggest, most magnificent, most popular royal event ever. One coronation that probably was as popular as made out to be — since it marked the return of the monarchy after the protectorate of Cromwell — was that of Charles II (page 50). The king entered London on his thirtieth birthday amid 'celebrations such as the capital had never known. Over 20,000 horse and foot soldiers brandishing their swords and shouting with joy, the way strewn with flowers, the bells ringing, the streets hung with tapestry, fountains running with wine.'

The day before the crowning, the king travelled by barge from Whitehall to the Tower of London loudly cheered by throngs lining the embankment. The next day, a sunny and beautiful St George's Day, April 23, 1661, still more crowds arose at dawn and hurried to find a good position along the route of the procession which was to wind its way from the Tower down to Whitehall and Westminster Abbey.

Four Sergeants at Arms on horseback led the brilliant procession. The Dukes of Normandy and Aquitaine came next, followed in turn by the Gentleman Usher with the black rod, the Lord Mayor of London, the Duke of York, the Earl of Lindsey, Lord Great Chamberlain of England, the Earl of Suffolk, and then the king himself, wearing a soft black hat with huge red and white ostrich feathers and surrounded by equerries and Gentlemen Pensioners. Finally came the Duke of Albemarle, Master of the Horse, and the Vice Chamberlain, the Captain of the Pensioners and the Captain of the Guard.

Samuel Pepys, who wrote at such length about the manners and morals of the Restoration court was up so early that morning that he claimed his seat way up in the scaffolding of the abbey at 4 a.m., and was half famished when the royal procession arrived seven hours later. He could not contain his excitement as he viewed the glittering panorama of nobles and peers of the realm in their parliamentary robes, the bishops in cloth of gold, the band of musicians in vests of blinding scarlet and then Charles looking every inch a king. When the Archbishop of Canterbury placed the crown on the king's dark flowing curls up went the deafening 'royal shout'. But Pepys was even more taken aback when the Treasurer of the Household started throwing silver coins up and down the aisle. His only regret, of course, was that he 'could not come by any'.

One of the strangest coronations in history must have been that of Napoleon in December 1804. After all, the last king, Louis XVI, and his queen Marie Antoinette, had been guillotined to the triumphant cries of *Vive la Republique* barely eleven years earlier, and a great many remembered it. But the proud self-made emperor, fully aware of the powerful effect that pageantry had in arousing a worshipful public, used it on every possible occasion, glorifying France and himself at one and the same time. After all, he was France's Caesar, the greatest military leader of the most powerful country and empire in Europe — enough justification, surely, for showing off in a big way. When the time came for his coronation in the cathedral of Notre Dame, Napoleon wanted it to be the most dazzling affair in the history of France, if not of mankind. None too well versed in royal protocol, he employed the diplomat, Louis Phillippe de Ségur, who had served at several European courts, to be his Grand Master of Ceremonies. At the same time he ordered an unwilling Pope Pius VII to travel all the way from Rome to be present for the occasion.

By the time everyone, including Napoleon, had taken a hand in 'transforming' Notre Dame both inside and out, one exhausted helper on his way out of the cathedral, when stopped and asked how the decorations were going on inside, sighed 'So much work has been done that God himself would lose his bearings.'

When the day came, inclement weather greyed the long and colourful procession that escorted Napoleon and Josephine — in the state coach drawn by eight white horses — through the streets of Paris to the cathedral. The entire lower half of Notre Dame had been decorated with a temporary covering of neo-Gothic design incorporating a large letter 'N' on each column.

Napoleon had decreed that Josephine's train should be carried by his sisters who, after much anger and tears at the idea of their sister-in-law being raised to a higher social rank than their own, were finally forced to agree. But when on the way up to her throne, Josephine stumbled at the first step, those nearby said they saw one of the sisters, all three of whom were as insensitive and rude as their brother, give the train a tug, hopeful no doubt that Josephine would fall flat on her face.

At the height of the proceedings Napoleon caused utter consternation by intercepting the crown as it was being handed to the Pope and haughtily crowned himself. And then, turning his back again on Pius VII he crowned Josephine (page 91). At another point in the proceedings, Napoleon yawned, and leaning toward his uncle Joseph Fesch, Cardinal and Archbishop of Rouen, nudged him with his gold sceptre, and was overheard whispering 'if only our father could see us now'.

The final insult was Napoleon's refusal to take communion from the Pope. When the artist Jacques Louis David, who had been commissioned to record the proceedings, showed Napoleon the result — which had taken him three years to complete from the many sketches he had made during the service — the emperor approved of it all except for the position of the Pope's hand. He wanted the hand repainted higher so that it looked as if Pius VII had raised it in a blessing.

The most unpromising of coronations was surely that of George IV, which in fact turned out to be an enormous success. The Prince of Wales, or 'Prinny' as he came to be nicknamed, was greatly disapproved of for tor devoting his life entirely to the pursuit of pleasure. At the age of fifteen his tutor, Bishop Richard Hurd, predicted that George would either become 'the most polished gentleman or the most accomplished blackguard in Europe — possibly both'. He did become both, and his scandalous spendthrift ways, if not actually contributing to the illness of his father, George III, certainly did not help to calm him in his growing distress.

A continuing drama right up through the coronation of George IV centred around his wife, Caroline. In desperation George III had nominated Caroline, his brother's daughter, in order that his oldest son could produce a direct and legitimate heir to the English throne. Nine years earlier, young George, or Prinny, had already been secretly married to Maria Anne Fitzherbert, with whom he had become infatuated and who was able at least partially to rescue him from 'those Pavilions of Pleasure where honour is not known'. The trouble was that the widowed Mrs Fitzherbert was a Roman Catholic and the Act of Settlement decreed that an heir apparent automatically forfeited all right to the crown by marrying one. But another Act made any marriage contracted by a member of the royal family under twenty-five invalid unless concluded with parental approval. And as his father had no idea at the time that he had actually married Mrs Fitzherbert, this 'mistake' could be dismissed as if it had never happened at all. When Prinny was yet again in deep debt, for an even greater sum of money than usual, George III agreed to bail him out once more, but only on condition that he married a decent and royal Protestant like Caroline.

Two more totally unsuited partners could not have been chosen, and shortly after the wedding in 1795 both rebounded in opposite romantic directions. While Prinny was handsome and had style 'on the scale that rivalled the Bourbons', Caroline was plain, blousy and in many people's opinion, quite 'dotty'. However, the couple managed to have a child in remarkably short order, Princess Charlotte being born in January 1796. Soon afterwards the two agreed to separate, not, however, without much bitterness on the part of Caroline. The Princess of Wales, who came to live mostly abroad, began taking pleasure in making an exhibition of herself to the point of shocking the whole of Europe — not so much because of immorality but because of her childish behaviour, sillinesses of dress and things of that kind. As one after another account of unprincessly behaviour was reported back to Prinny, she was delighted. 'I love to mortify him,' she would say.

When George III died, Prinny was the king and Caroline the queen of England. She was then living with a handsome bewhiskered Italian, Bartolomeo Bergami (she called him Pergami because it sounded more aristocratic and then Baron de la Francine, which sounded even better).

Caroline returned to London as England's new queen in June, 1820, and was not altogether unhappy to find herself the focus of the scandal of the century. She had many loyal supporters.

Complaining that Caroline had made him ridiculous 'from Lake Como to Jericho', Prinny (who was by no means guiltless himself) decided to charge her with adultery. At the trial her Italian servants were brought to London to give evidence, arousing enormous public interest. But in the end the proceedings became so ludicrous and distasteful that the case against Caroline was dropped.

Caroline thought she had won. But when she went to Westminster Abbey to see her husband crowned (as she had been hoping to be too) she was not allowed in, on the grounds that she had no ticket! Caroline died, strangely enough, only nineteen days later, not, as a few of her friends claimed, of a broken heart, but from an abdominal constriction which first hit her when she was watching a play at the Theatre Royal, Drury Lane.

Meanwhile Prinny had become an almost reformed character at Carlton House. Supported by his current favourite, Lady Conyngham, he even took a crash course in theology so as to prepare himself for the big event of July 19, 1821.

Contributing to the enormous success of the coronation was the fact that the last one, that of George III, had taken place sixty-one years earlier and very few people had any idea of what a truly magnificent spectacle the crowning of an English monarch was.

The excitement started after midnight of the day before when every half hour bells were rung and guns fired in salute, reaching its climax just after 10 o'clock at Westminster Abbey. All the honoured guests had then to wait for twenty-five minutes because his Lord Great Chamberlain, Lord Gwydyr, had somehow managed to stick his foot through his magnificent robe and tear it so badly that it took all that time to pin his lordship together sufficiently for the glittering procession to continue on course.

The king, wearing a Spanish hat with white ostrich plumes above his curly wig, making him look like some 'gorgeous bird of the East', trailed a twenty-seven foot train decorated with stars of gold. As he entered the Abbey he was greeted with the choirs' Hallelujah Chorus and loud shouts of welcome.

After a long and impressive service the royal procession moved under the covered walk to Westminster Hall to take part in the coronation feast, a medieval banquet and the last of its kind, at which three hundred and twelve guests in their robes of state settled down to tuck in (page 96). The provisions included: 160 tureens of soup, 160 dishes of fish, 160 hot joints, 160 dishes of vegetables, 480 sauce boats (lobster, butter, mint), 80 dishes of braised ham, 80 savoury pies, 80 dishes of goose, 80 dishes of savoury cakes, 80 dishes of braised capons with 1,190 side dishes. This was followed by 320 dishes of mounted pastry, 320 of small pastry, 400 dishes of jellies and creams, 160 dishes of shellfish (lobster and crayfish), 160 dishes of cold roast fowl and 80 dishes of cold lamb.

Following ancient tradition, during the first course, a young man — the king's champion — dressed in full armour and carrying a gauntlet rode into the hall on a white horse, and flung the gauntlet down three times as a challenge to anyone who denied that George was the rightful heir to the throne. No one did, of course, and with a good deal of merriment everyone turned his attention back to the meal.

While the banquet was an exclusive affair, the huge firework display in Hyde Park was for all to enjoy. Feasts were given throughout the country. Prinny had never been so happy — or so popular — in all his life.

Richard II dining with
Dukes of York and
Gloucester. From
Froissart's *Chronicles*.
English, 15th century.
British Library, London.

Royal banquet

Throughout European history — and still today
— meals were made into state occasions, often
signalling moves of diplomatic importance. Here
Richard II, seated beneath the royal canopy, is
entertaining two of his uncles, the Dukes of York
and Gloucester. Gloucester had been a persistent
critic and opponent of the king and was
eventually to be murdered at Calais on his
nephew's orders. This kind of feast would have
consisted of at least three courses, each offering a
prodigious choice of meat, fish, game, poultry,
pies, sweetmeats and jellies. Bread is on the table
and there were butts of ale and wine as needed.
The servitor in the foreground is carrying a *nef*,
an ornamental vessel in the form of a ship whose
use is still in dispute: did it hold cutlery, or the
salt, or was it an alms dish for offerings to the
poor at the king's gate?

17

Splendour and excitement

Tournament at St Inglevert. From Froissart's *Chronicles*. English, 15th century. British Library, London.

February, from a Flemish calendar, c.1500. British Library, London.

By the end of the fourteenth century, jousting was no longer a life and death struggle, but the most chivalrous of princely sports. The scene above is at St Inglevert, on the chalk down between Calais and Boulogne. Here, according to the chronicler, Jean Froissart, 'Three knights of great renown jousted for thirty days long amidst great splendour and excitement.' The two knights in the foreground, riding caparisoned horses, will take part in the joust, separated by the fence behind them. The audience gathers at a discreet distance.

Opposite: **Besides the holy days** set down in a calendar, any special occasion could be the excuse for a feast. The illumination here, showing a nobleman with family, friends, servants and entertainers, was made for the month of February in a Flemish calendar. It might well have been intended for Shrove Tuesday, the last day before Lent and forty days of fasting. In the bottom left-hand corner crouches the jester in motley.

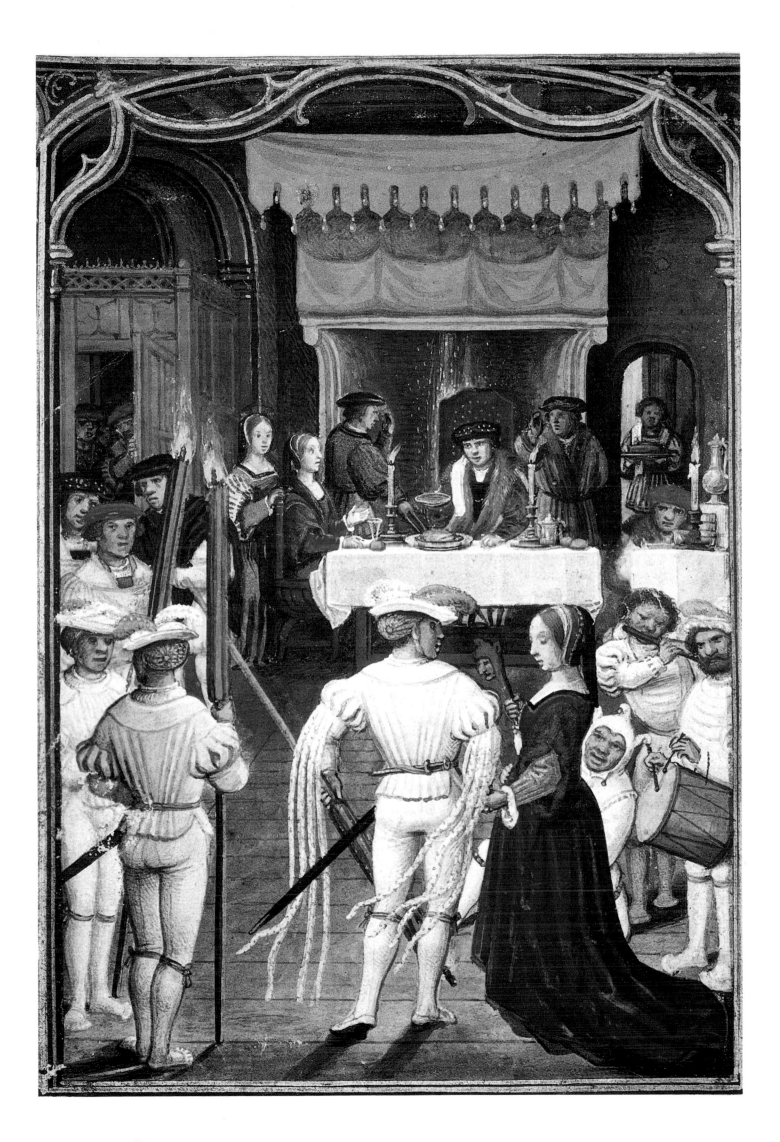

The pleasures of chivalry

King John of France was so greatly impressed with England's Order of the Garter — founded by Edward III in 1346 — that he wanted his own grand order of Knights. On 6 November 1351, he created the Order of the Star and celebrated the event with this feast. The King was 'Prince' of the Order which was made up of five hundred knights. Each was entitled to wear the huge star and to enjoy the benefits of a military club — with insurance and pension rights thrown in. But unlike Edward's still flourishing Order of the Garter, John's Order disappeared in the reign of his son, Charles V.

Knights of the Star at the Table of Honour. From *Grandes Chroniques de France.* French, 14th century. Bibliothèque Nationale, Paris.

May, from the Très Riches Heures du Duc de Berry. Limbourg Brothers. French, 1413–16. Musée Condé, Chantilly.

Few medieval princes could equal the elegance of the Duc de Berry and his fashionable entourage, no matter at which of his seventeen magnificent palaces the duke happened to be in residence. Here, on the first day of May, he is out with a party celebrating the festival of 'the full flowering of Spring' – hence the 'gay-green' dresses and crowns and garlands of leaves. The duke himself is probably the man in the left foreground; next to him, also turning back to look at the first girl in green, is a man dressed in black, white and red, the royal livery, possibly a prince of the blood. Behind the wood rise the fairy-tale towers of the Palais de la Cité in Paris.

21

Detail of Dido's feast and
hunt. Panel painting
attributed to Apollonio di
Giovanni. Italian, 15th
century. Niedersächsisches
Landesmuseum, Hanover.

Renaissance dream world

The small Italian courts present an intriguing mixture of cruel reality and seductive make-believe, often calling on the services of painters, poets and designers to provide settings that evoked the legends of antiquity. This detail from a panel attributed to Apollonio di Giovanni ostensibly represents the banquet given for Aeneas by Dido. But it is in fact an idealized picture of a Renaissance feast. The prince and his family sit at a table on a dais. Other guests are placed below. On the right items of gold plate are displayed on a sideboard.

Venice en fête

No city staged more dramatic spectacles than Venice. The ceremony of the 'healing of the demoniac' as depicted by Carpaccio in 1495 is typical of the grand pageantry to which its citizens were accustomed. A procession is moving across the Rialto Bridge as festively attired gondoliers row their elegant patrons across the Grand Canal toward the crowded loggia. Above, at the far left of the balcony, Archbishop Grado holds a fragment of the True Cross with which he is exorcizing a demon from the victim swaying before him. The whole picture is full of unexpectedly realistic details, from the washing suspended on poles from the roofs to the fluffy dog in the boat bottom right.

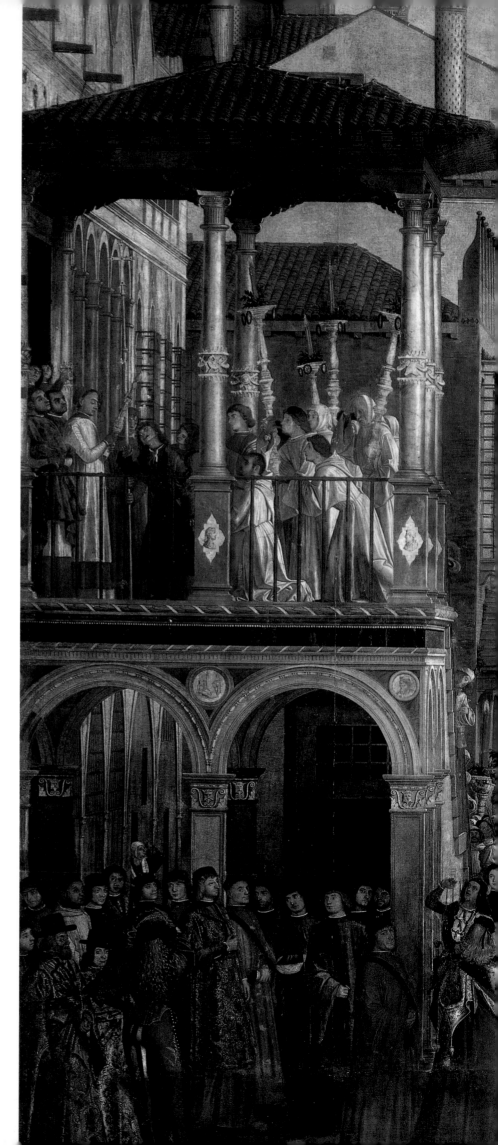

The Healing of the
Demoniac. Vittore
Carpaccio. Italian, c.1495.
Galleria dell'Academia,
Venice.

24

Scenes from the *Triumph of Maximilian,* made for Maximilian I. German, 1518. Graphische Sammlung Albertina, Vienna.

The imagery of power

Maximilian I, German king and emperor, employed several artists to illustrate a Roman style pageant honouring his political and military achievements. The resulting document, a cycle of 137 woodcuts and 109 miniatures, might well have served as a model for a real-life celebration had Maximilian lived longer. The details here are typical. Equestrian soldiers (*above left*) pass in review carrying banners of territories which in the emperor's eye, if not in fact, owed him allegiance

– Naples, Jerusalem, Sicily and Aragon. *Left*: a map displaying bird's-eye views of his chief fortified sites. *Above*: celebrants carry model ships representing Hapsburg victories on rivers and seas. Except as a popular folk hero, historians have never treated Maximilian well. Nevertheless, largely through the profitable marriages he arranged, the Hapsburg dynasty was to become under his grandson Charles V by far the greatest power in Europe.

27

The jousts of Florence and Venice

Tournament in Venice.
Domenico Morone. Italian,
15th century. National
Gallery, London.

28

Florence rivalled Venice as a city of pageantry and, on May Day, the official opening of the festival season, the revelry got off to a lively start. For two whole months Florence treated itself to a succession of tournaments, processions, bizarre masques, concerts and wedding feasts. The climax of the festival came on 24 June, the day of Saint John the Baptist, Florence's patron saint, customarily reserved for a mammoth firework display. The jousting knights here were known to the officials and the others in the balcony by the names embroidered on their bridles. Proceedings have reached the stage known as the mêlée, a sort of general free-for-all. Distinguished spectators watch from the windows of the houses behind. Ordinary folk look over the fence in the foreground, standing on benches to get a better view, or in one case crouching underneath them to peer through a hole in a plank.

Tournaments to match those in Florence were held at Carnival time in Venice's fabulous Piazza San Marco (left). Ranges of seats covered with a canopy have been specially built for the judge and members of the Venetian nobility.

Overleaf: **The Field of the Cloth of Gold**
One of the most glamorous spectacles in history, 'The Field of the Cloth of Gold', took place when two young kings — Henry VIII, twenty-nine, and Francis I, twenty-six — met near Calais in June 1520. France wanted a firm alliance with its traditional enemy, England, as a show of strength against the powerful Hapsburg Emperor Charles V. No expense was to be spared in impressing the English, so Jean Bourdichon designed a magnificent city of tents woven with threads of gold. Not to be outdone, Henry had crossed the Channel with an entourage of 5,000 and enough material to throw up 800 brightly coloured pavilions and tents. He is seen on the left of the painting leading the English contingent, with Cardinal Wolsey riding just behind. Directly above is Guines Castle, headquarters of the French. On the right is the palace put up by the English and covering 12,000 square yards, a building of 'mythical glory', with a fountain of wine. The festivities lasted three weeks with jousting (top right), wrestling (top centre), music, dancing and quantities of food, ale and wine. But nothing but golden memories ever came of all this. Within two years England had signed a treaty with Charles V and once again was at war with France.

Tournament in the Piazza Santa Croce. Master of the Jarves Cassoni. Italian, 15th century. Yale University Art Gallery.

29

The Field of the Cloth of Gold. Attributed to Vincent Volpe (or Fox). English, 16th century. Reproduced by gracious permission of Her Majesty the Queen.

Musical Party. Detail of a
painting on a virginal
made by Hans Ruckers.
Flemish, c.1586.
Metropolitan Museum of
Art, New York.

An afternoon concert in a Flemish Garden. The
instruments the musicians are playing are flutes,
lutes and shawms, double-reeded instruments
much used in the Middle Ages. Musical parties,
indoors or out, continued to be among the more
leisurely forms of princely entertainment
throughout all of Europe.

Opposite: **During the sixteenth century**, mock
battles became an enormously popular sport at
royal fêtes. The French King, Henry III, seen on
the right with his queen, Louise de Lorraine-
Vaudemont, chose 'The Age of Discovery' as the
theme for this palace garden skirmish. The
'savages' occupying the island in the background
are being given a lively time by the attacking
'Europeans', some of whom are dressed as
Romans, others in costumes of the day.

Overleaf: **A royal wedding**
Again at the court of Henry III, a grand ball
given on 24 September 1581 to celebrate the
wedding of Marguerite of Lorraine to the Duke
of Joyeuse, Admiral of France. The king, wearing
a tiny crown, is seated under the canopy on the
left. Next to him is his widowed mother,
Catherine de Médicis, and behind her, the sinister
Duke of Guise, or 'Scarface', head of the awesome
Catholic League. In the centre of the ballroom the
married couple dance to the music of Henry's
'mignons'. The king was severely criticized for his
love of clothes, his dandyism and for the
effeminacy of his court. Needless to say, the
nation's textile industry loved his extravagant
ways.

Nautical games at the
court of Henri III. Brussels
tapestry after a cartoon by
Antoine Caron, c.1580.
Galleria degli Uffizi,
Florence.

Ball at the court of Henri III for the wedding of the Duc de Joyeuse and Marguerite de Lorraine.
Attributed to Herman van der Mart. 16th century. Musée National du Château de Versailles.

Detail from Queen
Elizabeth I and members
of the Order of the
Garter. Engraving after
Marcus Gheerearts, 1576.
Reproduced by gracious
permission of Her Majesty
the Queen.

Elizabeth, mistress of ceremonies

Queen Elizabeth I, daughter of Henry VIII and
Anne Boleyn, lived on the flattery of her subjects
and promoted her own image by every device of
costume and jewelry. Here, sparkling with rubies,
diamonds and pearls, she is being transported in
her richly embroidered palanquin to Blackfriars,
where her pretty maid of honour, Anne Russell, is
to be married to Lord Herbert. The bride is on
the right. Her father, the Earl of Worcester, is the
knight wearing a pink doublet and garter. In front
of Worcester are other Knights of the Garter.
Early in her reign, the young queen (above) waits,
bouquet in hand, to meet a procession of
members of the Order of the Garter. In the
background is Windsor Castle. The date is 1576.

36

Procession of Queen
Elizabeth I. Attributed to
Robert Peake. English,
c.1600. Private Collection.

A medieval festival in Siena's main piazza, the
Campo, was full of the 'usual' surprises — dragons
and other mythological creatures (activated by
humans hidden inside them) stealing the show —
or trying to — from the bull and bear baiters.
Siena has seventeen Contrades, or districts, each
with a symbolic animal customarily represented
on occasions like this.

Festival in the Campo,
Siena, Vincenzo Rustici.
Italian, c.1600. Courtesy
Monte dei Paschi, Siena.

A tourney in Siena's Piazza del Campo,
honouring Ferdinand I, de' Medici, Grand Duke
of Tuscany, the much loved grandson of Lorenzo
the Magnificent. Imposingly displayed in the
foreground are the family arms of the noble
competitors.

Tournament in Siena in
honour of Ferdinand I.
Italian, 1607–10. Archivio
di Stato, Siena.

Spring picnic. Lucas van
Valkenborch. Flemish,
1587. Kunsthistorisches
Museum, Vienna.

The court on holiday

In summertime a 'simple' feast was often carried
out of doors. Among the many points of interest
to be enjoyed by the picnickers here are the

winding river and island maze, the distant city
and the joust taking place in front of the palace.
Lucas Van Valkenborch, recently from Holland,

made a series of these paintings around 1585
while he was working for Archduke Matthias, and
staying near Vienna.

Two princely marriages

Fairy tale pageantry with three gaily decorated floating pavilions, makes an unusual double wedding on the beautiful Bidasoa all the more remarkable. In 1615, Philip IV of Spain, aged ten,

married Louis XIII's sister Isabel, aged thirteen, and at the same time Louis XIII married Anne, the sister of Philip IV – both aged fourteen. So as brother and sister married sister and brother, the two young princesses became queens; helping to cement diplomatic relations between the two countries facing each other across the river. Philip succeeded to the throne in 1621, aged sixteen.

Exchange of brides on the River Bidasoa. Spanish, c.1615. Museo de la Encarnación, Madrid.

43

Cills dann diß alls ein ende nam,
Vnd man von kirchen hainwarts kham,
Da ward allßbald ein Kayßerlich,
Pancket berait, herrlich costlich,
Vnd alßen beieinander ßgleich,
Der Kayßer sambt den fürsten reich.

A gathering of Hapsburgs

Rudolf II at a banquet in
Prague. German, 17th
century. Österreichische
Nationalbibliothek, Vienna.

It is said that 'no Hapsburg ever died of excess food or drink' – or indeed 'ever died of laughter'. Rudolf II lived up to both maxims. But the frugality and sternness of the emperor eased up at times, especially in the company of guests who could share his passion for science. The astronomer Tycho-Brahe and his younger colleague Johannes Kepler were friends who stayed with Rudolf at the Castle in Prague where he had set up court in preference to Vienna. But on this occasion the emperor is seen entertaining his uncles, the Archdukes Ferdinand, Charles and Ernst along with his courtiers. Rudolf is seated at the head of the table, on the left, and food is being served on the right, behind the musicians.

The Triumph of Isabella

The fantastic Ommeganck in Brussels was an annual festival held in honour of the Virgin Mary. But on this occasion, 31 May 1615, the queen of the fête was the Archduchess Isabella, consort of Archduke Albert, Belgium's equally popular ruler. The setting is Brussels' Grande Place, through which the procession winds in a double S-bend. The two double-pages that follow show the left and right halves.

Overleaf: In the background are four brightly caparisoned camels ridden by children; the third has been transformed into a unicorn and the fourth into a dragon. Next comes a cart representing Christ among the Doctors. In the middle row, after a company of soldiers, comes the Nativity. In the foreground the main cart, on the right, carries a huge birdcage and a man seated on a throne surrounded by attendants dressed in feathers; he is King Psapho of Libya, an oriental potentate who taught birds to speak his name. At the end of the procession come more camels.

Following page: Starting again at the back, first comes a cart showing the virtues of Isabella ('Heroina Isabella') and then an elaborate ship carrying figures of the Virgin and Child – it is towed by sea-horses and followed by sea-elephants pulling the Pillars of Hercules. (This cart is particularly interesting as it was made for the funeral of Charles V some sixty years earlier.) In the middle row we see the Annunciation; the stem of Jesse, with King David under a canopy from which grows the Tree ending in the Virgin; and Apollo and the Nine Muses. The two carts in the foreground represent the Court of Isabella, with Fame seated on a pillar, and Diana and her nymphs.

Ommeganck. Denis van Alsloot. Flemish, 1616. Victoria and Albert Museum, London. (See description, pages 44–45)

Ommeganck. Denis van Alsloot. Flemish, 1616. Victoria and Albert Museum, London. (See description, pages 44–45)

Charles II at a ball in the Hague. Janssens. Flemish, mid-17th century. Reproduced by gracious permission of Her Majesty the Queen.

Ball for an exiled king

King Charles II, in princely dress, leading his sister, Mary, at a ball in the Hague. Their mother, Henrietta Maria, is seated in the group behind them. After the royalist defeat in 1651 Charles went into exile in France, but from 1656 onwards he lived in the Netherlands — at Brussels, Bruges and Breda. Oliver Cromwell died in 1658; the Puritan Commonwealth crumbled and Charles, whose existence in exile had become increasingly penurious — though never unromantic — was brought home in 1660 to be crowned, 'amidst celebrations such as the capital had never seen before'. Although the so-called Merry Monarch of the Restoration was to be soundly condemned for the looseness of his morals, no English sovereign did more to foster the arts or was more tolerant of critical writers with opposing philosophies.

Pageant for an exiled queen

Queen Christina of Sweden, daughter of the
Protestant hero Gustavus Adolphus, abdicated the
throne in 1654, became a convert to Catholicism
and took up residence in Rome in December
1655. Here she lived in great state, and soon
after her arrival – in February 1656 – this
spectacular entertainment was mounted in her
honour. It featured a mock battle between
Cavaliers and Amazons. The setting is the
courtyard of the Palazzo Barberini. The queen
watched from the lower of the two red boxes in
the centre. *Above*: a similar 'loge' with ladies on a
balcony watching the Feast of the Four Altars in
Rome.

Detail from the Feast of
the Four Altars. Niccolo
Maria Rossi. Italian, 17th
century. Private
Collection.

Pageant in honour of
Queen Christina of
Sweden at the Palazzo
Barberini, c.1656. Lauro e
Gagliari. Italian, c.1656.
Museo di Roma.

Detail from *Courses de festes et baque faites par le Roy et par les princes et seigneurs de sa cour*. Jacques Bailly. Costumes designed by Henri de Gissey. French. c.1670.

In 1662 Louis XIV of France, then aged twenty-three, assumed absolute power. To mark the occasion a particularly splendid entertainment was mounted. 'Drowned in vanity', the king set out to show the world that 'Paris could surpass the best of whatever was being done elsewhere.' There were 650 horsemen dressed in fantastic costumes the most prominent of which were the 'Romans', led by the king, and the 'Indians' (shown here) led by the Duc de Guise.

The Man of Ice. French,
1651. From *Ballet du Roy
des Festes de Bacchus*, 1651.
Bibliothèque Nationale,
Paris.

Two costumes for *The Festivals of Bacchus*, a
spectacular show staged at the Palais Royale
when Louis was only twelve. It included music,
dancing and spoken dialogue. Two of the more
exotic characters are the Man of Fire and the
Man of Ice, seen here. The whole play is full of
subtle – and not so subtle – allusions to the
young king and the fact that he will soon grow
up and be popular with the ladies.

The Man of Fire. French,
1651. From *Ballet du Roy
des Festes de Bacchus* 1651.
Bibliothèque Nationale,
Paris.

Château and garden of Versailles. Pierre Patel. French, 1668. Musée National du Château de Versailles.

Seat of the 'Sun King'

Early in the 1660s Louis XIV began thinking of developing his favourite retreat, his father's palatial hunting lodge, into what he envisioned as the largest and grandest palace in Europe. Finally in 1668, after impressing upon Louis le Vau that he wished no expense to be spared on the renovations, he approved the architect's magnificent plans. Forty years of noisy construction and muddy landscaping followed before the enlarged Versailles was ready for the king to move into with his entire court and hundreds of government officials. Here in 1688 he is seen arriving at Versailles with his queen, Marie-Thérèse, and courtiers for one of his last festive visits before the transformation began. The king is in the red coach drawn by six horses and preceded by his mounted cavalry. The queen is in the second coach. The smaller picture (*above*) shows the king in his carnival costume of the previous page.

The court on tour

In 1667 Louis XIV went in person with his queen Marie-Therèse, courtiers and military personel to view the battleground after the Siege of Lille. All are dressed as if for a great spectacle at court. The queen is in the coach. Louis follows on a white horse. Probably on this occasion Louis' mind was preoccupied more with domestic problems than with military ones: both Louise de la Vallière and Madame de Montespan were also of the party, the latter as the queen's lady-in-waiting. Before they returned to Paris la Vallière had ceased to be the king's mistress and Montespan had taken her place.

Entry of Louis XIV into Arras. Francois Van der Meulen, 1667. Musée National du Château de Versailles.

Nymphenburg Castle.
Bernardo Bellotto. Italian,
1761. National Gallery of
Art, Washington.

Masked ball at the theatre
of Bonn. Franz Jacob
Rousseau. German, 18th
century. Ministry of
Culture for North Rhine-
Westphalia, Düsseldorf.

The world of Rococo

In the 18th century the small German courts
took over some of the brilliance and variety that
had characterized Italy in the past. This colourful
regatta with Venetian gondolas (*above*) is taking
place in the grounds of the palace of
Nymphenburg just outside Munich, the summer
residence of the Electors of Bavaria. It was said
that at times the gondoliers would increase the
fun of their passengers by making them think
they were about to be splashed by the fountain,
and then steering them away in the nick of time.
The palace, which bears a certain resemblance to
Versailles, was started in 1663 and then added to
in 1712. It is viewed here as Bernardo Bellotto,
the nephew and pupil of Canaletto, saw it in
1761 when he was painting views in and around
Munich. *Right*: a glittering masked ball in the
eighteenth century attended by Bonn's élite – and
one pet dog – at the city's lovely Baroque
theatre. The magnificent costumes include native
German, French, English, Venetian, Russian and
Chinese.

Venetian Carnival

As Venice's political power waned, the city became the pleasure capital of Europe, famous — or notorious — for its Carnival where the conventional rules of society were forgotten and

every excess permitted. This painting of the Piazza S. Marco during the Carnival shows various activities which could hardly co-exist: in one corner bull-baiting with dogs, in another a performance by *commedia del'arte* players. On balconies, in windows, underneath arcades lurk masked figures engaged in who knows what secret intrigues?

Carnival in the Piazza San Marco. Francesco Heinz II. German, 17th century. Galleria Doria Pamphili, Rome.

63

'Bride of the Adriatic'

The early rulers of Venice had named their city the Adriatic's bride because their livelihood depended on the shiploads of cargo the sea helped bring in. Their gratitude to the benevolent

'spouse' was expressed annually in the festival *'Sposalizio di Mare'* or 'Marriage to the Sea'. The ceremony was conducted by the reigning Doge who, after boarding the gold state barge (seen here in the background on the right) and leading a procession of gondoliers to the lip of the lagoon, ceremoniously tossed a wedding ring into the waters and led prayers for a happy union.

The Feast of the Ascension. Giovanni Antonio Canal, called Canaletto. Italian, 1730. Private Collection.

'A season of madness'

Venice at festival time was a 'city of masks'. Noble ladies flirted behind black *moratas*, or half-masks, their male counterparts behind white birds-beak masks. Giovanni Domenico Tiepolo's painting is of Venetian society in the eighteenth century at carnival time. A desperate, nostalgic, almost ghostly feeling underlies the gaiety of the nobility at play, as if they are all feverishly trying to rekindle the spirit of a nobler, happier past. Immorality and crime in Venice finally reached such depths that the government's Council of Ten put a stop to the Carnival once and for all.

The Minuet. Giovanni Domenico Tiepolo. Italian, mid-18th century. Musée du Louvre, Paris.

In 1744, at St Peter's in Rome, Pope Benedict XIV greets Charles III, King of Naples and Sicily, following his victory at Velletri. Charles had just defeated the Austrian army there, halting their proposed advance and occupation of Naples.

Some twenty years later, after his half-brother Ferdinand VI died, Charles became King of Spain and was painted (above) dining 'in public' with members of his Spanish Court. The huge state rooms of the Royal Palace in Madrid were still the setting for elaborate ceremonial and rigid etiquette, but Charles, who was sympathetic to the Enlightenment, laboured to reform the Spanish administration and reduce the despotic power of the Church.

A king's progress

The entry of Charles III to the Vatican. Giovanni Paolo Pannini. Italian, 1744. Museo di Capodimonte, Naples.

Charles III at table. Luis Paret y Alcazar. Spanish, c.1700. Prado, Madrid.

The eternal city transformed

Coaches splash through two feet of water in the Piazza Navona in Rome. This unique spectacle is believed to have originated in a small way following an exceptional downpour in Rome. The Piazza was then often flooded on purpose, offering the gentry an interesting change of pace from the uneventful *passeggiata* they usually took through the city. The fun reached its climax toward the middle of the eighteenth century when Pannini made this painting. It came to an abrupt end when the square was levelled. Today's young Romans love to go hooting through the 'dry' piazza in their Fiats and other flashy cars.

Piazza Navona flooded.
Giovanni Paolo Pannini.
Italian, 1756.
Landesgalerie, Hanover.

Arrival of an infant king

Overleaf: **The excitement in front** of the Sainte-Chapelle in Paris is caused by the arrival of the five-year old Louis XV who, dressed in white, is being carried under the wide central arch. In 1715 he had succeeded his great-grandfather, Louis XIV, under the Regency of Philippe II d'Orléans, and now enters the chapel to confirm the regent's appointment. The thirteenth-century Saint-Chapelle, built as a shrine for France's most holy relic, the Crown of Thorns, still stands unaltered, but is now surrounded by the buildings of the Palais de Justice.

Louis XV outside the
Sainte-Chapelle. Pierre-
Denis Martin. French,
1715. Musée National du
Château de Versailles.

71

The oyster feast. Jean-François de Troy. French, 1737. Musée Condé, Chantilly.

Louis XV at home

Louis XV was twenty-seven when De Troy painted this scene for his apartments. The bachelor party is predominantly of young men about the king's own age, and from descriptions of Louis, it is easy to image him as one of them. Not only is the luxurious oyster and champagne feast typical of the high style of living at Louis' Rococo court, but the clothes epitomize the height of male fashion towards the middle of the eighteenth century. The artist was obviously intrigued with the idea of painting the young gourmet opening a bottle of bubbling champagne so he could also depict the cork up in mid air.

Louis' mistress, the extremely bright, talented and pretty Marquise de Pompadour — on the right — was not only the king's confidant, but an influence in guiding his policies from 1745 until she died in 1764. Her favourite artist, François Boucher, painted the famous portrait of her below. Though of a slightly later date, her dress is the perfect counterpart to the male fashions painted by De Troy.

Madame de Pompadour. François Boucher. French, 1758. National Gallery of Scotland, Edinburgh.

'Le Bal des Ifs'

A magnificent costume ball given at Versailles' Galérie des Glaces in 1745 to celebrate the wedding of the Dauphin to Maria Teresa, daughter of Philip V of Spain. One of the eight topiary trees – modelled after the yews in the palace gardens – is Louis XV in fancy dress. The other seven 'yews' are his courtiers. Other courtiers on the right are dressed as Turks with

enormous turbaned heads. It was here that Madame d'Etioles — later the Marquise de Pompadour — dressed not inappropriately as the 'Huntress', Diana, first met the king. Seeing one of the 'yews' approaching and guessing it to be the king, Diana dropped her handkerchief. The king, obviously charmed by the beauty of the 'huntress', picked it up.

Le Bal des Ifs. Nicholas Cochin. French, 1745. Cabinet des Dessins, Musée du Louvre, Paris.

The theatre takes over

In the Baroque era, the distinction between celebration, spectacle, and theatre became blurred, and as theatres themselves grew larger, richer and more highly decorated they were increasingly used as the settings for public occasions. Here the Teatro Argentina, in Rome, built in 1732, displays a huge architectural set as a backcloth for a princely entertainment, organized in 1747 by the French ambassador, Cardinal La Rochefoucauld, to celebrate the wedding of the Dauphin to a princess of Saxony. The Cardinal and his distinguished guests, who included James Edward Stuart, are seated on the stage, surrounded by musicians. A cantata by N. Jommelli was performed. Important members of the audience have armchairs in the front; hundreds more crowd into the pit, boxes and galleries.

Musical fête in the Teatro Argentina, Rome. Giovanni Paolo Pannini. Italian, 1749. Musée du Louvre, Paris.

79

The end of war

The firework display in Paris on 21 June 1763
was an expression of happy relief that the Seven
Years' War, which had cost France so dearly, had
finally come to an end. That far-flung conflict
made Prussia, under King Frederick II, the
foremost military power in Europe, and England,
under the political leadership of the brilliant
young William Pitt, the leading colonial power.
Peace treaties had been signed at Hubertusberg
Castle in Saxony, as well as here in Paris.
Although France had yielded vast territories in
Canada and America, Parisians, shrugging their
shoulders, lit up the skies of their beloved city in
a show of patriotism. The sign, 'Vive le Roy',
honouring Louis XV — though he was largely
responsible for the country's losses — blazes in
the elaborate skeleton of a temple across the river
Seine.

Firework display in Paris.
L.N. Van Blarenberghe.
French, 1763.

Wedding of a Hapsburg heir

Carousel de Dames.
Marten van Meytens.
Swedish, 18th century.
Kunsthistorisches Museum,
Vienna.

Concert in the
Redoutensaal. Marten van
Meytens. Swedish, 18th
century. Kunsthistorisches
Museum, Vienna.

Entry of the Bride into
Vienna. Marten van
Meytens. Swedish, 1760.
Kunsthistorisches Museum,
Vienna.

For forty years, from 1740 to 1780, the vast
Hapsburg empire was ruled by a woman, Maria
Theresa, the daughter of Charles VI. It was not
an easy reign, but by skill, dedication and
shrewdness she overcame her difficulties and left
the empire strengthened and intact to her son,
later Joseph II. Joseph's wedding to Isabella of
Parma was made the excuse for a series of
celebrations that surpassed anything that had
been seen for decades. The couple were married
by proxy in Parma; the bride entered Vienna in
October 1760. Her procession, shown *overleaf* in
a schematized form doubling back upon itself in
front of the Hofburg, was long and splendid.
Isabella is seated in the gold carriage in the
foreground.

Above: Carousel de Dames, or ladies' tournament,
in the Spanish Riding School at Vienna's Imperial
Palace. The lofty Baroque building was designed
for Maria Theresa's father by the renowned
Austrian architect Fischer von Erlach. The
Empress, a noted horsewoman herself, led several
of these highly stylized tournaments. Some ladies
of the court are riding in carriages, others are
mounted on the white Lippizaners, for which the
Riding School is still famous.

Opposite: Among the many wedding
entertainments arranged for Joseph and Isabella
was an opera party at the candlelit Hofburg
Redoutensaal, where Johann Hasse's *Alcide in
Bivio* was performed.

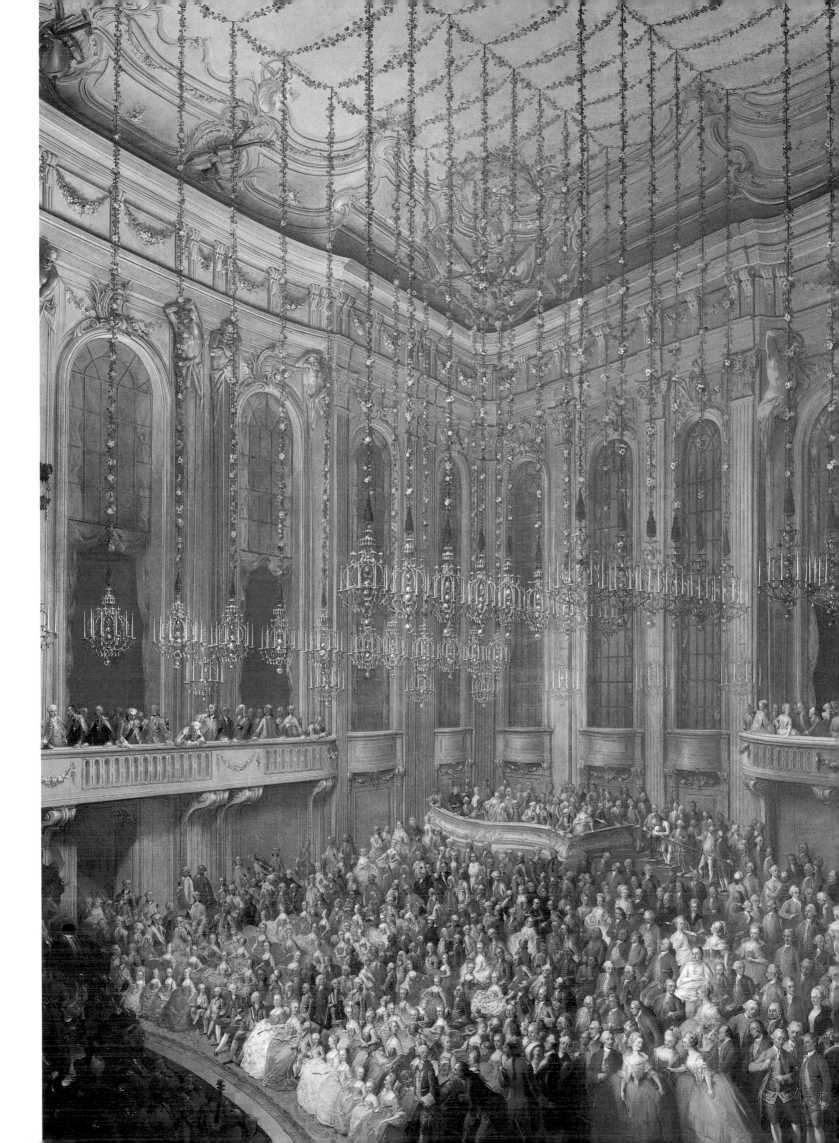

The Lord Mayor
proceeding to
Westminster. Richard
Paton and Francis
Wheatley. English, 1789.
Bridgeman Art
Library/Guildhall Art
Gallery, London.

The Lord Mayor goes to Westminster

London's renowned Lord Mayor's show had its beginnings in 1215 when the chosen citizen had to journey to Westminster to be approved officially by the king. Until the fifteenth century the Mayor was obliged to walk or ride there on horseback, but later it became the fashion to go by boat. Here, in the reign of George III, spectators watch from the banks of the Thames as gaily bedecked barges, many richly carved and painted, escort the Lord Mayor with customary pomp and circumstance, down river to Westminster. Rising in the background are the spires of Wren's City churches, and the mighty dome of St Paul's Cathedral, completed some eighty years earlier, replacing the medieval church destroyed in the Great Fire of 1666.

Last lights of the Ancien Régime

As the French economy worsened and murmurs of rebellion grew louder, Louis XVI and his queen, Marie Antoinette, retreated from affairs of state into their own private world of Versailles. And when even that became too formal they took refuge in the charming garden buildings such as the Petit Trianon and the Hameau. Here a fête is in progress around the Belvedere, a little octagonal summer house finished only in 1781. Eight years later the lights were to go out for ever.

Fête at night in the gardens of the Petit Trianon. Claude Louis Chatelet. French, 1781. Musée National du Château de Versailles.

The Emperor Napoleon.
Jean-Dominique Ingres.
French, 1800. Musée de
l'Armée, Paris.

The Coronation of
Napoleon. (Detail).
Jacques-Louis David.
French, 1804, copy made
in 1822. Musée National
du Château de Versailles.

The new empire

It is one of the paradoxes of history that the
French Revolution – fiercely anti-monarchist and
republican – should in little more than a decade
have led to an imperial regime even more
powerful than the one it replaced. Jacques-Louis
David and Jean-Dominique Ingres have
immortalized Napoleon's glory. In Ingres' portrait
he poses like a classical Jupiter holding the
attributes of kingship. David's great painting of
his coronation in Notre Dame, Paris, in December
1804 depicts the moment when the Emperor,
after crowning himself in front of Pope Pius VII,
turned and placed a crown on the head of his
wife Josephine.

Overleaf: Napoleon and his second queen, Marie-
Louise, the daughter of Francis II of Austria,
entering the Tuileries after their wedding. In 1810
Napoleon divorced Josephine because she had not
produced the desired heir, and married into the
most powerful of the old European royal families.
The heir was born – made King of Rome in his
cradle – but never inherited his empire.

Napoleon and Marie-
Louise ariving at the
Tuilèries. E.-B. Garnier.
French, 1810. Musée
National du Château-de
Versailles.

'The Prince of Pleasure'

In 1820 the Prince Regent, who had already reigned for ten years on behalf of his mentally ill father George III, succeeded to the throne as George IV. He had a reputation for loose morals, high living and luxury, but also for a quality of imagination that distinguished him from other Hanoverians. His Royal Pavilion at Brighton had been designed by John Nash to satisfy his hankering after the exotic. The Banqueting Room (previous page) was an oriental fantasy, its dome filled with giant plantain leaves beneath which a Chinese dragon supported a chandelier in which smaller dragons held lamps shaped like lotus flowers. In this illustration the Prince himself sits on the right, reaching for the wine. His

Coronation banquet in Westminster Hall in 1821 (above) was almost as fantastic. The old tradition of the King's Champion was revived and he is seen entering on horseback on the right accompanied by attendants dressed in Jacobean costume.

Previous page: Banqueting Room at the Royal Pavilion, Brighton. From John Nash, *The Royal Pavilion at Brighton*, 1827.

Coronation banquet of George IV. John Whittaker and George Naylor. English, 1821. From *The Ceremonial of the Coronation of King George the Fourth*, 1821–41.

Revels and recipes: an anthology

The following collection of texts, drawn from historical records, literature, cookery books and other sources, is intended to show, by direct quotation, how eating and drinking, entertainments and festivals have been seen by different people at different times and in different places during the period covered by this book.

Pygges in sawse sawge

Take pigges yskaldid and quarter hem, and seeth hem in water and salt; take hem up and lat hem kele. Take persel, sawge, and grynde it with brede and yokes of ayren harde ysode; temper it up with vynegar sumwhat thyk, and lay the pygges in a vessell, and the sewe onoward and serve it forth.

> sawse = sauce
> sawge = sage
> kele = cool
> persel = parsley
> ayren = eggs
> ysode = boiled
> sewe = juices
> onoward = on top

The Forme of Cury, 14th century

Pantomime pastry

Make a terrace of brown bread and make the figure of a damsel seated on the terrace, which should be covered with a sheet of tin stained green so as to look like a grassy meadow.

You then need a lion, who can stand either with his head and front paws or his back to the damsel. He should have a brazen mouth and a long brazen tongue, and the teeth can be of paper pasted to this mouth. Here you put camphor and a wick of cotton, and when it is served before the lords, set light to it.

From the *Vivandier* of Guillaume Tirel, known as Taillevent, mid-14th century.

A Renaissance dinner party

They returned to the house, where they found that Parmeno had made a diligent beginning with his office, for that, entering a saloon on the ground floor, they saw there the tables laid with the whitest of cloths and beakers that seemed of silver and everything covered with the flowers of the broom; whereupon, having washed their hands, they all, by command of the queen, seated themselves according to Parmeno's ordinance. Then came viands delicately drest and choicest wines were proffered and the three serving-men, without more, quietly tended the tables. All, being gladdened by these things, for that they were fair and orderly done, ate joyously and with store of merry talk, and the tables being cleared away, the queen bade bring instruments of music, for that all the ladies knew how to dance, as also the young men, and some of them could both play and sing excellent well. Accordingly, by her commandment, Dioneo took a lute and Fiammetta a viol and began softly to sound a dance; whereupon the queen and the other ladies, together with the other two young men, having sent the serving-men to eat, struck up a round and began with a slow pace to dance a brawl; which ended, they fell to singing quaint and merry ditties. On this wise they abode till it seemed to the queen time to go to sleep, and she accordingly dismissed them all; whereupon the young men retired to their chambers, which were withdrawn from the ladies' lodging, and finding them with the beds well made and as full of flowers as the saloon, put off their clothes and betook themselves to rest, whilst the ladies, on their part, did likewise.

Giovanni Boccaccio: *The Decameron,* 1453

The Wedding of Charles the Bold and Margaret of York

The tables were laid in the same way as for dinner, but they were much larger, and on the said tables were thirty vessels in the form of ships, each bearing the name of one of the lordships of my lord of Burgundy, among which were five duchies and fourteen counties; the rest were the lordships of Salins, Malines, Arcle and Bethune, great and noble estates. The said vessels were painted gold and azure, and bore the arms of the lordships from which they were named on their banners, shields and masts; of which each vessel had three, flying the banners of my lord of Burgundy, and at the very top a great black and violet silk standard, sewn with golden lozenges, and in large letters was the motto of my lord the Duke: 'Je l'ay emprins'. The food was inside these ships, which served as dishes. The sails were of silk and all the rigging was gilded with fine gold. Model men-at-arms and sailors had been made and stood among the ships and everything was so true to life that one could distinguish a carrack from a great ship.

Item, on the said tables were thirty great patés covered with lids in the form of great tall castles, all painted gold and azure and carrying the banners of my lord of Burgundy; and on each of the castles were the arms and name of a fine city owned by my lord; and in this way were displayed thirty principalities and lordships that were part of my lord the Duke's heritage, and thirty towns that were subject to him, without parallel in the world.

Item, for the furnishing of these tables, each vessel had round it four smaller boats containing richly dressed fruits and spice.

Item, three pageants were presented between the courses, of which the following was the first.

First a unicorn as big as a horse entered the room, covered with a silk caparison painted with the arms of England; and upon this unicorn was a leopard, extremely well made and very lifelike. This leopard held a great banner of England in its left hand and in its right a marguerite, very well made. And after the said unicorn had paraded in front of the tables to the sound of trumpets and bugles, it was led up to the Duke and one of his stewards took the said marguerite from the said leopard, and kneeling before the said Duke spoke these words:

'Most excellent, high and victorious prince, my most dread and sovereign lord, the proud and dread leopard of England has come to visit this noble company, and for the consolation of you, your allies, lands and subjects, presents you with this noble marguerite.' And thus the said Duke received the said marguerite very cordially, and the said unicorn went back the way it had come.

Memoires d'Olivier de la Marche, 1468

The Field of the Cloth of Gold

Thursdaie the viii daie of June being Corpus Christi daie the king of England and the ffrenche king mett in a valley called the goulden dale which dale lyeth in the midwaie betwixt Guisnes and Arde in which Arde the frenche king laie during the triumph. In the said dale the king had his pavilion of cloth of gould pight where there was a certein banquett prepared for the said kings the kings grace was acompanied with five hundred horsmen and three thousand footemen. In like wyse the french king was accompanied with a great company of horsemen and footemen: at the tyme of the meating of theis ii renowned Princes there was proclamacouns made on both parties by the heraults and officers of arms that everie companye should stand still the kind of England with his companie on the one side of the dale and the frenche king on thother side in likewise: then proclamacouns made paine of death that every companie should stand still till the two kings did ride downe the valley and in the bottome they meett where ever of them embrased other on horsbacke in great amytie and then incontinent they lighted from their horses putting their horses from them and imbrasing other with their capps in their hands. . . .

Sondaie the xxv daie of June the ffrench king dined at Guisnes with the Queene of England accompanied with xxviii lords and more besides ladies and gentilweomen which were a great nomber which were apparaled in masking clothe with vizards on their faces gorgiouslie beseene and likewise at the same tyme the king of England dined with the ffrench Queene at Arde with xl lordes ladies and gentilweomen specially his owne naturall sister marie the ffrench queene dowagier of ffrance which the Duke of Bourbon like a noble prince desired and did serve her grace of her cupp with all honour and reverence to him possible which Lords and Ladies were richlie apparaled in masking clothes of cloth of tissue of gould and cloth of silver and in the storie of the kings maske was the life of Hercules.

From a contemporary account of the meeting of Henry VIII and Francois I, 1520

The Gastrolators: worshippers of gluttony

In this order, they moved towards master Gaster, after a plump, young, lusty, gorbellied fellow, who, on a long staff, fairly gilt, carried a wooden statue, grossly carved, and as scurvily daubed over with paint; such a one as Plautus, Juvenal, and Pomp. Festus describe it. At Lyons, during the Carnival, it is called Maschecroute, or Gnaw-crust; they call this Manduce.

It was a monstrous, ridiculous, hideous figure, fit to fright little children: its eyes were bigger than its belly, and its head larger than all the rest of its body: well mouth-cloven however, having a goodly pair of wide, broad jaws, lined with two rows of teeth, upper tier and under tier, which, by the magic of a small twine hid in the hollow part of the golden staff, were made to clash, clatter, and rattle dreadfully one against another; as they do at Metz, with St. Clement's dragon.

Coming near the Gastrolaters, I saw they were followed by a great number of fat waiters and tenders, laden with baskets, dossers, hampers, dishes, wallets, pots, and kettles. Then under the conduct of Manduce, and singing I do not know what dithyrambics, crepalocomes, and epenons, opening their baskets and pots, they offered their god,

White hippocras, with dry toasts.	Fricassees, nine sorts.	Cold loins of veal, with spice.
White bread.	Monastical brewis.	Zinziberine.
Brown bread	Gravy soup.	Beatille pies.
Carbonadoes, six sorts.	Hotch-pots.	Brewis.
Brawn.	Soft bread.	Marrow-bones, toast, and cabbage.
Sweet-breads.	Household bread.	Hashes.
	Capirotades.	

Eternal drink intermixed. Brisk delicate white wine led the van; claret and champaign followed, cool, nay, as cold as the very ice, I say; filled and offered in large silver cups. Then they offered,

Chitterlings garnished with mustard.	Scotch collops.	Hogs' haslets.
Hams.	Puddings.	Brawn heads.
Hung beef	Carvelats.	Powdered venison, with turnips.
Sausages.	Bolognia sausages.	Pickled olives
Neats' tongues.	Chines and peas	

All this associated with sempiternal liquor. Then they housed within his muzzle,

Legs of mutton with shalots.	Plovers.	Fried pastry-crust.
Olias.	Dwarf-herons.	Forced capons.
	Teals.	Parmesan cheese.

Lumber pies with hot sauce.	Duckers.	Red and pale hippocras.
Ribs of pork with onion sauce.	Bitterns.	Gold-peaches.
Roast capons, basted with their own dripping.	Shovelers.	Artichokes.
	Curlews.	Dry and wet sweet-meats, seventy-eight sorts.
	Wood-hens.	
Caponets.	Coots, with leeks.	Boiled hens, and fat capons marinated.
Caviare and toast.	Fat-kids.	
Fawns, deer.	Shoulders of mutton with capers.	Pullets with eggs.
Hears, leverets.	Sirloins of beef.	Chickens.
Partridges and young partridges.	Breasts of veal.	Rabbits, and sucking rabbits.
	Pheasants and pheasant poots.	Bacon pies.
Quails, and young quails.	Stock-doves, and woodculvers.	Hedgehogs.
Pigeons, squabs, and squeakers.	Pigs, with wine sauce.	Snites.
		Then large puffs.
Herons, and young herons.	Blackbirds, ousels, and rayles.	Thistle-finches.
Fieldfares.	Moor-hens.	Whores' farts.
Olives.	Bustards, and bustard poots.	Fritters.
Thrushes.	Fig-peckers.	Cakes, sixteen sorts.
Young sea-ravens.	Young Guinea hens.	Crisp wafers.
Geese, goslings.	Flamingoes.	Quince tarts.
Queests.	Cygnets.	Curds and cream.
Widgeons.	A reinforcement of vinegar intermixed.	Whipped cream.
Souced hog's feet.		Preserved myrabolans.
Mavises.		Jellies.
Grouse.	Venison pasties.	Welsh barrapyclids.
Turtles.	Lark-pies.	Macaroons.
Doe-conies.	Dormice-pies.	Tarts, twenty sorts.
Peacocks.	Cabretto pasties.	Lemon-cream, raspberry cream, etc.
Storks.	Roe-buck pies.	
Woodcocks.	Pigeon pies.	Comfits, one hundred colours
Snipes.	Kid pasties	
Ortolans	Capon pies.	Cream wafers.
Turkey cocks, hen turkey.		Cream-cheese.

Vinegar brought up the rear to wash the mouth, and for fear of the squinsy: also toasts to scour the grinders.

François Rabelais: *Gargantua and Pantagruel*, 1546

Conduct to be avoided

The upper servants, who wait at table, must in no circumstances scratch their heads or other parts of the body in front of their master when he is at dinner, nor should they touch any of the parts of the body which are normally covered. They should not even look as if they were touching them, as some careless servants do when they tuck their hands in the top of their aprons or clasp them behind their backs under their coat-tails. They must hold them where they can be seen, so that no one need be apprehensive, and they must keep them washed and scrupulously clean without the least trace of dirtiness about them.

Those who serve the dishes or pour the wine must take care not to spit or cough, and still more not to sneeze, while they are performing these duties. It is just as objectionable for the diners to suspect the waiters of such conduct as actually to witness it, and since a supposed misdemeanour is as aggravating as a real one, servants should be on their guard not to give their masters cause for suspicion.

It is bad manners to clean your teeth with your napkin, and still worse to do it with your finger, for such conduct is unsightly. It is wrong to rinse your mouth and spit out the wine in public, and it is not a polite habit, when you rise from the table, to carry your toothpick either in your mouth, like a bird making its nest, or behind your ear. Anyone who carries a toothpick hung on a cord around his neck is certainly at fault, for besides the fact that it is a strange object to see drawn from beneath a gentleman's waistcoat and reminds us of those cheapjack dentists who can be seen in the market-place, it also shows that the wearer is well equipped and provided with the wherewithal of a glutton. I cannot explain why these people do not also carry their spoons tied around their necks.

I do not think it right to offer food from one's own plate to anyone else, unless the person who offers it is of much more exalted rank, in which case it would be a mark of honour for the other. If both are of equal rank it is rather a presumption of superiority for one of them to offer his food to the other, and sometimes the titbit might not be to his taste. It also shows that the dishes were unfairly served, since one person has too much and the other not enough, and this might embarrass the host. Nevertheless, in this matter we must do as everyone else does, and not as we think right. In conventions of this sort it is better to be wrong in company with others than to be the only one to be right. But whatever may be the rights of the matter, you must not refuse what is offered to you because, if you do, you will appear to despise or rebuke the person who offers it.

Giovanni Della Casa, *Galateo*, 1558

Banquet for a Queen of France

... She was conducted by a specially made gallery leading from the door of the church to a magnificently painted and decorated staircase, which she ascended to reach the great hall prepared for her reception. Here she was greeted by a fanfare of trumpets, bugles and cornets, testifying to the immense joy felt by everybody at her coming ...

Her majesty having for some time contemplated the beauties of the room, she was presented with water to wash her hands, and her waiting women likewise. She then took her place at the table where she was served with as many kinds of rare and exquisite fish, according to the season, both from the sea and from river, as could be wished.

The Prévôt des Marchands acted as steward; after him came gentlemen and officers of his household carrying dishes, preceded by more trumpets and bugles.

There were four other tables for the lords, ladies, gentlemen and maidens who were present, and for them the Echevins performed the same office of steward, followed by the Enfants de la Ville carrying the meat; they were dressed as they had been the day before. The service was so well managed, so excellent and varied, that the lords and gentlemen testified that they had never in their lives seen anything like it.

... The King was equally pleased; he was present with his brothers and several princes and great lords, who were all filled with wonder at the novelty of this banquet.

Among which, in addition to the infinite number of preserves of all sorts, both dried and bottled, the variety of sweets, quince paste, marzipans, biscuits and other rarities that were there, the guests saw with amazement a display of every sort of fruit that could be found in the world, whatever the season, and plates with every sort of meat and fish – all made of sugar! It was so natural that many people were actually deceived; even the dishes and bowls containing them were made of sugar!

Diner offert à la Reine par la Ville de Paris dans la grande salle du Palais Episcopal, 30 Mars, 1571

Montaigne questions his steward

... an Italian, whom I have lately entertained into my service. Who during the life of the whilom cardinal *Caraffa* served him in the place of steward of his house. Enquiring of his charge, and particular qualitie, he told me, a long, formall, and eloquent discourse of the science or skill of epicurisme and gluttonie, with such an Oratorie-gravitie, and Magistrale countenance, as if he had discoursed of some high mysterious point of divinitie, wherein he hath very methodically decifred and distinguished sundrie differences of appetites: First of that which a man hath fasting, then of that men have after the first, the second, and third service. The severall means how sometimes to please it simply, and other times to sharpen and provoke the same; the policie and rare invention of his sawces: First, in general terms, then particularizing the qualities and severall operations of the ingredients, and their effects: The differences of salades according to their distinct seasons, which must be served in warme, and which cold: The manner how to dresse, how to adorne, and embellish them, to make them more pleasing to the sight. After that, he entred into a large and farre-fetcht narration, touching the true order, and due method of service, full of goodly and important considerations.

> — *Nec minimo sanè discrimine refert,*
> *Quo gestu lepores, et quo gallina secetur.* — *Sat. v. 127.*
> What grace we use, it makes small diff'rence, when
> We carve a Hare, or else breake up a Hen.

And all that, filled up and stuffed with rich magnificent words, well couched phrases, oratorie figures, and patheticall metaphors; yea such as learned men use and imploy in speaking of the Government of an Empire.

Michel de Montaigne: *On the Vanity of Words*, 1585

To make Hodge Podge

Take a piece of beef, fat and lean together, about a pound, a pound of veal, a pound of scrag of mutton, cut all into little pieces, set it on the fire, with two quarts of water, an ounce of barley, an onion, a little bundle of sweet-herbs, three or four heads of celery washed clean and cut small, a little mace, two or three cloves, some whole pepper, tied all in a muslin rag, and put to the meat three turnips pared and cut in two, a large carrot scraped clean and cut in six pieces, a little lettuce cut small, put all in the pot and cover it close. Let it stew very softly over a slow fire five or six hours; take out the spice, sweet-herbs and onion, and pour all into a soup dish, and send it to table; first season it with salt. Half a pint of green peas, when it is the season for them, is very good. If you let this boil fast, it will waste too much; therefore you cannot do it too slow, if it does but simmer.

Eliza Smith, *The Complete Housewife*, 1766.

Republican manners

1. When you are at table, sit up straight on your chair, without leaning over or stretching in a careless or negligent way. Do not put either your arms or your hands on the table, and take care not to poke your neighbour with your elbow. It is always rude to scratch in company, but especially at table. There are people who keep staring avidly at the food as if they wanted to devour it with their eyes: try to avoid this appearance of gluttony.
2. Do not hold out your plate too eagerly to be served first, but wait your turn; and if you are offered a dish, do not take the nicest pieces for yourself, above all if there are older people or ladies to be served after you.
3. Do not eat too slowly, nor too fast, and do not fill your mouth with such large pieces that chewing becomes a problem.
4. Do not lean over your plate too much. Bend down slightly when you are drinking, but then sit up again straight away.
5. Good manners require that you cut your bread with a knife, and put meat in your mouth with one hand only and with the fork.
6. Avoid touching anything greasy, or sauce, etc. with your fingers, because this obliges you to be constantly wiping your hands on your napkin, which soon becomes dirty, or wiping them on a piece of bread, or licking them — all things which are extremely ill-bred if one is eating in company.

7. Do not put the bread on the plate or on the table to cut it, and do not eat the crust separately from the crumb.

8. When you are at table, eat well and as much as you want. On the other hand, do not eat more than you really need. Moderation is one of the paths to health.

9. Before and after drinking remember to wipe your mouth, and do not fill your glass too full in case you spill it.

10. Drink calmly, and be sure not to drink with your mouth full. Take care also when drinking not to make a noise in your throat so that everybody can count how many mouthfuls you have swallowed.

There are many other more detailed rules that you can easily learn by practice and by following the example of well-brought-up people.

Chemin-Dupontès, *La Civilité Republicaine*, 1798

Banquet scene; woodcut
by M. Wohlegemut for
A. Koberger's 'Der
Schatzbehalter',
Nuremberg, 1491

Index

Page numbers in *italics*
refer to illustrations

Photographic Acknowledgments

References are to page-numbers

Lauros-Giraudon, Paris 72–73; Mas, Barcelona 69; Réunion des musées nationaux, Paris 34–35, 58–59, 78–79, 92–93; Scala, Florence 24–25, 38, 39, 62–63, 64–65

Quadrille de
Mr. le Duc
D'Anguien

Monsie
grand

Quadrille de
Monsieur le
Prince

Quadrille